About the Auth

I am Alessandro Lazzara, IT technician with over 10 years of experience in this sector. I decided to write this little guide for those who like you, do not digest technology very much, or are novice, and want to learn how " repair your pc yourself ".

Prologue

It must be said that, if your PC has a failure, making many unsuccessful attempts without knowing what to do, can be counterproductive both for the health of the computer and for the protection of the data inside it, so OK try to resolve, but with some moderation.

In this book I will show you how to solve many of the most common problems, those things that block most novice people; (this guide will not help you solve 100% of the faults, precisely because sometimes there can be much more serious and complex problems, which necessarily need the intervention of an expert in the matter).

Chapters:

The computer does not turn on

Windows

If your computer shows no signs of life and therefore if you press the power button, nothing happens (no lights, no noise, no signal on the video), it is very likely that the electricity is not coming to your PC.

How do you know if that's the problem?
Easy, if it is a fixed PC, check that the power socket is connected well, that the cable is intact, and that the power extension (if it is connected to a power extension) is working, in case it tries to change the power socket for safety.

While if yours is a portable PC, check that the external power supply (the black box) is connected well on both the socket and the Notebook side, and that the power extension and socket work well.

Mac

Press the Mac's power button. All Macs have a power button, usually marked with the power symbol, then check for power signs such as:

Sounds, such as a fan or hard drive, or another startup sound

Lights, such as a backlit keyboard, the Caps Lock key or the stop light

If your Mac shows no signs of power, first check that it is powered:

Make sure the power cord is intact and securely connected to the Mac and a working electrical outlet. If you have any doubts about how the outlet works, try it with a lamp or other device.

If you're using a Mac notebook, make sure you're using the correct power adapter and power cord and make sure your computer has been plugged in for about 5 minutes, which is enough time to provide sufficient battery power.

If you use an external display, make sure it is turned on and connected securely to your Mac and that there are no video or display problems.

Then try these solutions, regardless of whether your Mac shows signs of power or not:

Hold down the Mac's power button for 10 seconds, then press it again.

Reset the system management controller (SMC).

Make sure the display brightness is turned on. The Increase brightness button is available on the integrated keyboard of Mac notebook computers.

Disconnect all accessories from the Mac, including printers, drives, USB hubs and mobile devices (the problem may be with one or more of these devices or their cables). Hold the power button for another 10 seconds, then press it again.

If your Mac shows signs of power, but the screen remains blank, try following the necessary steps when the Mac shows a blank screen on startup.

Black screen

Windows

It can happen, and it usually happens when you really need the PC, that the Computer after giving the normal initial signs of life (the fan turns, the lights come on ...) shows up with a completely black screen.

No Windows loading, no start page, no cursor, in some cases after a few seconds the word "No Signal" may appear (which comes from the monitor and not from the PC).

In this case the problem could be due to the malfunction of the video card, the one that sends the signal to the monitor or to another internal component connected to it.

But you can try to do one thing.

If yours is a fixed PC try to unplug the PC power cable, then hold the power button for 30 seconds, release the button, reconnect the cable and start the PC again.

If, on the other hand, you have a portable PC, try to disconnect both the power cable and the battery (if possible), then hold the power button for 30 seconds, release the button, reconnect everything and restart the PC.

If even so you don't solve the problem, you will have to turn to a technician who does a more accurate analysis and fixes it.

Mac

If the monitor turns off, your Mac or monitor may have stopped. If you have a laptop, it may have run out of energy.

The computer and monitor may have stopped

If the screen goes black and returns to normal when you press a button or click the mouse or trackpad button, the Mac or the screen has gone to sleep. To save energy, the Mac and monitor automatically sleep when not in use. You can put Mac and monitor to sleep at different times. Since the monitor wakes up faster than Mac, you generally set the monitor to sleep before Mac.

The laptop may have run out of charge

If the laptop monitor turns off, but has not entered sleep, it may have run out of energy.

Connect the power adapter to the computer and to a power outlet.

Disconnect any device that is connected to the computer except the power adapter.

Hold down the Command and Ctrl keys while pressing the power button to restart the computer.

Allow the battery to charge at least 10% before connecting any device to it and start working again.

Check the power and cables: make sure the power cable is connected to the computer and to a working power outlet. On laptops, the power adapter plug turns yellow if the battery is charging and green when the battery is fully charged. Make sure you're using the power adapter that came with your computer or a compatible replacement adapter. If that doesn't work, try another cable or power adapter to see if the problem is with the power supply or the computer itself.

If you have a portable Mac with a removable battery: you can check if the battery needs to be recharged by pressing the button on the battery or on one side of the computer. To find out where the button is located, consult your computer's documentation. You should see lights that indicate the battery charge level. If only one of the lights is flashing, have the adapter recharge the battery as long as the light stays on continuously.

If you still can't start it, your Mac may need assistance.

How to install and manage updates

Currently Windows 10 provides a notification center where it updates users on all updates of the operating system and installed programs. The only problem is that it does not warn the user when he is downloading the updates.

For this reason, sometimes, after turning on the computer, you can find the blue screen that warns of the installation of some files: very often it lasts only a few minutes, instead other times it is necessary to wait even ten or twenty minutes, a precious time lose at work.

Few are aware of the opportunity to schedule a computer restart in a more congenial moment: just enter the Settings, click on Update and Security and then on Restart Options. A window will open that will allow the user to decide the time of the next updates, without fear of restarting the computer during working hours.

How update my Mac

Have you just switched from Windows to macOS and would like some information on how the Apple operating system update system works? Are you trying to download an update from the Mac App Store but the operation is not successful due to an error and you don't know how to solve the problem? Don't worry, if you want, I'm here to help you out.

Take five minutes of your free time and I'll explain how to update Mac using different methods. We will therefore see how to update macOS (and the applications installed on the computer) using the special function of the Mac App Store, how to solve the download problems of the Mac App Store, how to take advantage of the Combo Updates released by Apple on its official website and, how to make a clean install of the latest version of macOS.

Do many of the names and terms that I have just listed you are obscure? Don't worry, if you're new to the Mac world it's normal. But now, for this reason, do not waste any more time and get to work immediately: take some free time, read the instructions I am about to give you and put them into practice to update your Mac to the latest version of macOS.

The easiest way to update Mac is to go to System Preferences, for system updates, and to the Mac App Store, for applications downloaded from the Mac App Store (those downloaded from external sites must be updated using the special function included in each of them).

So open System Preferences (the gear icon located on the Dock bar), choose the Software Update icon and wait for the search for the latest available system updates. If the presence of updates is detected, accept their installation by clicking on the Update now button and then following the instructions on the screen.

As for applications, you can check for updates by opening the Mac App Store and selecting the Updates item from the left sidebar. If updates are available for an app, click on the button to install them, which you should find next to the name of the application.

If you are using a version of macOS prior to 10.14 Mojave, you need to download both system updates and app updates via the Mac App Store. If configured appropriately, the Mac App Store can manage all updates automatically, in the sense that it can verify the availability of updates, can download them in the background and, at the end of the download, can offer the user their installation through the notifications that appear on the desktop.

At that point, the user can decide whether to proceed with the installation of the update (which usually requires a computer restart) or whether to postpone the operation by clicking on the appropriate buttons.

The update mechanism is the same both for intermediate updates (e.g. from macOS 10.12.3 to macOS 10.12.4) and for major upgrades (e.g. from macOS 10.11.x to macOS 10.12). However, installation times and methods change: intermediate updates are automatically installed in a few minutes (generally about fifteen) without user intervention. The major upgrades are installed through a special application that is downloaded to the Mac (e.g. macOS Sierra in the case of macOS 10.12) and require, at least initially, an intervention by the user, who must accept the conditions of use of the software and must select the target disk of the operating system. The installation times, as can be easily guessed, expand quite a bit compared to those of the intermediate updates.

How to configure automatic updates

If you want to set the automatic download of updates for macOS and / or for applications downloaded from the Mac App Store, open System Preferences (the gear icon located in the Dock bar), go to Software Update and, if it is not still present, put the check mark next to Keep your Mac updated automatically.

Next, click on the Advanced button and put a check mark next to all the available items: Check for updates (to activate the automatic search for updates), Download new updates when available (to start downloading updates), Install macOS updates (to activate automatic installation of updates), Install app updates from the App Store (to activate automatic installation of app updates) and Install system data files and security updates (to activate installation automatic critical security updates).

If you use a version of macOS prior to 10.14 Mojave, you have to follow a slightly different procedure: open System Preferences and select the App Store icon from the window that is shown to you on the screen. At this point, depending on your preferences, put or remove the check mark from the following options.

Check for updates automatically - to activate the automatic search for updates.

Download available updates in the background - to enable automatic download of updates. Install app updates

Install app updates - to activate the search and / or download of updates for applications downloaded from the Mac App Store (option available only by activating "Check for updates automatically").

Install macOS updates - to activate the search and / or download of updates for macOS (option available only by activating "Check for updates automatically").

Install system data files and security updates - to allow automatic installation of the most important security updates (recommended).

Install automatic updates

When macOS finds a system update and downloads it, it notifies you with a notification that appears at the top right of the desktop. At that point, as already explained, you can decide whether to proceed with the installation of the update or whether to postpone the operation a few hours later (e.g. in the evening) or the next day.

Then click on the notification button relating to the option of your interest, for example Install / Restart to install the update immediately or Later to postpone it, and proceed accordingly.
If you decide to install the update immediately, click on Download and restart, accept the conditions of use of macOS (if necessary) and wait patiently for the update to be installed on your Mac. The computer will restart and you will have to wait about 15- 20 minutes for the installation of the update to complete.

If, on the other hand, you decide to postpone the update, you do not have to do anything: you can continue with your work normally until macOS asks you again what you want to do with the available updates.

As previously mentioned, in the case of macOS major upgrades, the procedure to follow is slightly different. The application relating to the version of macOS to be installed on the computer must be downloaded (e.g. macOS Mojave in the case of macOS 10.14) and, at the end of the download, it must be started to accept the conditions of use of the software and select the disk target.

Updating the computer is a very important operation, I dare say vital. If you don't regularly update your PC's operating system, you will be much more exposed to viruses and hacker attacks. That's why today I decided to tackle the topic and to show you how to update your PC in a clear and simple way.

It doesn't matter whether you have a "classic" PC with Windows or a Mac, both systems are equipped with automatic update functions that keep your computer reasonably safe. Just understand how to use them and what they offer in detail. Are you ready to find out? Even if you are not very IT expert you will understand everything, promise!
Position yourself comfortably in front of your multimedia station and immediately start focusing on reading the following. In the end, I am sure, you will have perfectly clear ideas on what to do and you can say that you are happy and satisfied with what you have learned. Ah, I almost forgot: I will also give you some advice on updating the installed third-party programs that can in turn expose the computer to various risks and create malfunctions when obsolete.

If you want to find out how to update your PC and use the Windows operating system, you must rely on Windows Update which automatically downloads the most important updates for the Microsoft home operating system, the most updated versions of Internet Explorer and Edge (only on Windows 10) and corrective patches for Microsoft Office. It also downloads the definitions for the Microsoft Security Essentials antivirus and drivers for the supported hardware components.

The service works completely automatically by checking, downloading and installing all the critical Windows updates for you (do you know that window in the lower right corner that appears from time to time and asks you to restart your PC to install updates?) But if you want you can force the verification of the availability of any updates or you can change these settings easily.
In this case, the operations to be undertaken varying according to the version of Windows you are using. Below you will therefore find out how to proceed in detail.

Windows 10

If you are using Windows 10, access the Start menu by clicking on the button on the taskbar (the one with the Windows flag), click on Settings (the icon with the gear) and select Update and security in the window that appears on the desktop. Check that the Windows Update item is selected in the menu on the left (and if not, select it) then click on the Check for updates button to check if there are update packages available to download to your PC.
As an alternative to the button you could also see a specific item appear indicating that updates have already been identified and you must restart the computer or plan a restart.

If instead you want to change the mode and frequency with which new updates are searched for, downloaded and installed, click on the Advanced options item at the bottom then click on the menu under the wording Choose how to install updates and select the Notify option for scheduling the reboot instead of Automatic (which is the default). In this way, you will be asked to schedule a restart to complete the installation of the updates, while in the case of a consumer Internet connection, the updates will not be downloaded.

If you want to delay the download of updates for a few months, put a check mark next to the item Delay updates. If, on the other hand, you want Windows Update to also download updates for other Microsoft products installed on your computer, check the Download updates for other Microsoft products during Windows update box.
If you need to view the history of updates already made, select the wording View the history of updates always attached to the same window.

If you own more than one computer that you have connected to the same Microsoft account, I inform you that you can enable updates from multiple locations. In this way, you will download Windows updates from other PCs besides Microsoft and you can speed up the procedure in question. If you are interested in it, click on the Choose how to deliver updates item, turn the switch that appears to ON and select how to retrieve updates by choosing between PC in the local network or PC in the local network and on the Internet.

Windows 8.x / 8, 7 and Vista

If instead you are using Windows 8.x / 8, 7 or Vista, you can adjust the Windows Update settings to update the PC by clicking on the Start button (the one with the Windows flag) and look for the Control Panel in the Start Screen or in the Start menu that appears (depends on the version of Windows used).
Once the Control Panel window is displayed on the desktop, click on the System and security item and / or on Windows Update (depending on the type of view enabled). In the displayed screen, click on the Check for updates button to start the search for updates.

If Windows has already downloaded the latest updates for your computer, it will be indicated on the screen and you can therefore proceed with its installation.
If you want to change the settings related to the search, download and installation of updates, click on the Change settings item in the menu on the left.

Then expand the drop-down menu under the heading Important updates and select the option you prefer among those available: Install updates automatically (recommended) (it is the default), Download updates but allow the user to choose whether to install them , Check for updates but allow the user to choose whether to download and install them or Never check for updates (not recommended).

If you choose to leave automatic search enabled, you can decide on which days and at what time to install the new updates, using the appropriate menus next to the item Install new updates:

Please note that always in the same window you can decide, by putting or removing the check from the relevant boxes, whether or not to download the recommended updates in the same way as the imported ones and whether or not to allow the installation of updates on the computer for all users.
In all cases, remember to confirm any changes made, click the OK button at the bottom.

Update third part programs

As anticipated at the beginning, updating third-party programs installed on Windows is also very important. Unfortunately, the operation cannot be performed via Windows Update. To update the PC in this sense, it is therefore necessary to take advantage of the specific function to check the updates of the individual software.
In most cases it can be accessed from the program settings and from there the automatic detection of any new versions can also be enabled.

Customise or disable notifications

Windows

The notification center introduced in Windows 10 is certainly very convenient, but at the same time it can create problems for the user by slowing down computer processes.

If you do not consider the notification center to be fundamental for your user experience, Microsoft offers the possibility to disable some of its features: you will need to enter Settings, click on System and then click on Notifications and Actions.

A menu will open where you can enable or disable the different options depending on the functionality you need. To improve the speed of your computer, the first step is to disable notifications sent by applications developed by third parties.

Mac

View notifications in the Notification Center

To open Notification Center, click the drop-down menu in the upper right corner of the screen or swipe left with two fingers from the right edge of the trackpad.

To view missed notifications, such as Calendar alerts or FaceTime calls, click Notifications at the top of the Notification Center.

To open a notification in the app that sent it, click on the notification. The notification is then removed from the Notification Center.

To remove notifications without opening them, click the delete button next to a notification or group of notifications.

To show the Do Not Disturb and Night Shift controls, swipe up (or down) in the Notification Center.

To open the Notifications preferences, click the gear button in the lower right corner of the Notification Center.

Customize or disable alerts

Choose Apple menu □> System Preferences, then click Notifications.

Select an app in the left column.

To change the style of the notifications, select Banners or Alerts. Alternatively, select None.

You can also control other features here, for example if notifications are displayed on the lock screen or if they include a preview. A preview contains part of the email, chat or other content associated with the notification. You can choose to never show previews, to always show them or only when you unlock the Mac.

Use do not disturb

The Do Not Disturb feature mutes incoming notifications and calls. It activates automatically when the Mac is connected to a TV or projector.
To choose when to turn Do Not Disturb on or off, choose Apple menu (□)> System Preferences, then click Notifications. Do not disturb settings are available at the top of the sidebar.

Make your pc faster

Windows Defraggler

Although defragmentation is a useful process for your hard disk and, in general, for your computer, it is also true that many users often want to activate this feature or run it manually because it requires time, which is often not available.

Defraggler is a free software that meets this need, with a tool that allows you to defragment a partition of a PC or only the files that require it. In this way, the defragmentation times will be faster, with the possibility of forgetting them, if a programming has also been set.

If you are interested in downloading this software on your PC with Windows operating system, you can download it from the official website https://www.ccleaner.com/defraggler.

Reached the website from the link I provided, click on the Download Free Version button and then on Free Download. Then choose the mirror from where to download, such as CCleaner.com.

Once the file has been downloaded, double-click on it and then click the Yes button in the User Account Control window. After selecting the language, click on the Next button and then on Next. Uncheck the boxes for the features you don't want to enable and click Install and then Finish.
Once installation is complete, start the program and select one of the partitions that you see on the screen at the top of the Defraggler interface. Then click on the Analyze button, to start analyzing the state of the partition.

Once the process is completed, you will be shown the results of the analysis, indicating the percentage of fragmented files. Then click the button at the bottom Defragment to start defragmenting the partition.
You can also start a faster process (Rapid Defragmentation) which will allow you to carry out this procedure according to some preset rules, such as the one that ignores large files.
If instead you want to defragment only the files that need this procedure, you can click on the File List tab and select the files you want to defragment; you will then have to place a check mark next to the files you want to defragment and then click on the Defragment selected files button.

C cleaner

When the problems concern instead a failure to clean the computer from temporary and obsolete files, then CCleaner comes into play.

This free software can be downloaded both on operating systems with Windows and on those with macOS. To download it, simply go to its official website and then click on the Download button next to the Free column.

After downloading the installation file, double-click on it and then click the Yes button in the Windows User Control window. After starting the installation interface, click on the Customize item and remove the check mark from all those items you want to remove. Then click Install to begin the installation.

After starting the program, you will be immediately shown the CCleaner home screen. You will then have to evaluate what operations to perform based on the problem that is affecting your PC at the time.

Below I summarize the main features of this software:

Cleaning: allows you to remove temporary and obsolete files present on your PC, whether they are generated by your operating system or by the supported software installed on your computer.

Registry: if the Windows registry contains obsolete entries, CCleaner will clean it up.

Tools: this section of CCleaner contains some features that are intended to solve some common PC problems. You will then be able to remove software and applications, disable programs that run automatically, analyze the hard disk to locate large files.

Whatever the procedure you want to perform, I advise you to carefully follow the instructions on the screen, so as not to be sure of running into any problems.

Change some settings

If your PC is slow, you may want to consider turning off the animations and graphic effects that are used in the Windows interface. These elements, in fact, require the use of performance that on long-standing PCs could cause significant slowdowns.

Also consider not to apply changes to the themes or the Windows interface: often the third-party tools that allow the customization of the Windows interface could slow down the performance of your PC, especially if dated.

If you want to know how to disable Windows graphic effects, then read on the next lines. First, you will need to open the Windows Control Panel. To do this, in Windows 10 click on the icon with the symbol of a magnifying glass (Search) and type the term control panel.

Then click on the corresponding result and, from the window that has just opened, click on System and Security. Then click on System and then, from the items on the left of the window, on the wording Advanced system settings.
You will be shown a small window, where you will have to go to the Advanced tab and click on the Settings button, in the Performance section.
From the list of items that are shown to you, you will need to make sure that there is no check mark on Show previews instead of icons, Show window shadows, Save the previews of the taskbar, and Smooth the corners of the screen fonts.
Then click Apply and then the Ok button. I also recommend that you try disabling other voices and seeing the impact on your PC's performance.

You will also have to check that the indexing system of your PC is active and, if so, on which elements of your PC it acts. Indexing is the feature that allows you to search through the

Windows Search function and identify any corresponding elements.

If you have indexed all the items, folders and partitions of your PC, this could slow down the performance of your PC.
I therefore advise you to check which elements you need to index. To do this, click on Windows 10 on the icon with the symbol of a magnifying glass (Search) and type the term indexing options. Then click on the corresponding search result and, from the newly opened window, click Edit.
Then put a check mark on the elements you want to index and remove it from the superfluous ones. When done, click Ok and then Close.

Disable programs that run automatically

The slowdown on your PC can also result from the many programs that automatically run when Windows starts. In this case you will have to disable all those programs that you are sure are of no use to you when you turn on Windows.
To do this, you can rely on the use of third-party software, such as CCleaner, or the integrated functionality of Windows. Since there is no difference between one and the other tool, we therefore see the tools offered by Windows.

To do this In Windows 10, open the Task Manager, through the key combination CTRL + Shift + Esc OR CTRL + Shift + Esc. You can also open it, simply by right-clicking on the Windows Taskbar at the bottom and selecting the Task Manager item.

Then reach the Startup tab and disable all the on-screen services that are unnecessary according to your needs. Then right-click on one of them and select the Disable item.

How to speed up your Mac

Macs don't have all the typical problems of Windows computers. This is true.

For example, there is no system registry that can be "flooded" or filled with superfluous keys that slow down the functioning of the computer, are less subject to viruses and are not marketed with so many useless software (on board) (bloatware) as instead happens with Windows PCs. However they are not perfect and they are not without problems.

In other words, yes, Macs can also become slow; they can show error messages and even crash. In short, contrary to what the Apple marketing department wants us to believe are not "magical", but fortunately there are ways to speed up Mac and bring their performance back to the levels that would be expected from such expensive machines.

Which? You will find everything explained below, where a guide on how to speed up Mac where I tried to put together all the possible solutions to slowness problems on macOS (or previous versions) awaits you: read it and try to put it into practice. After following it all the way you should be able to fully exploit the potential of your Apple brand computer again.

Deactivate the applications set for automatic start

It doesn't take an IT expert to understand it: if the computer is forced to run a large number of applications simultaneously, whether it is equipped with Windows or with macOS (or earlier versions), it ends up slowing down.

This is why to speed up Mac and bring its performance to the maximum, it is necessary to disable the superfluous software set for automatic execution when the operating system starts. How you do it? Nothing could be easier.

Go to System Preferences by clicking on the gear icon contained in the Dock bar or looking for it in the Applications folder of the system and select the Users and groups item from the window that opens. In the screen that appears, make sure your user account is highlighted in the left sidebar and select the Login Items tab.

Then identify the applications you do not want to run automatically when the system starts and deactivate them by clicking first on their icons and then on the - (minus) button located at the bottom left.

Clear the cache files

Some minor malfunctions of macOS (and earlier versions) and some slight hitches in system performance can be caused by the presence, on the computer, of some corrupt cache files. To solve the problem you can use OnyX https://www.titanium-software.fr/en/onyx.html a precious free utility that allows you to reconstruct the cache files and customize some advanced aspects of the Mac.

To download OnyX to your computer, connected to the application's website, by clicking on the link that I have provided a moment ago, and click on the Download button relating to the version of OS X installed on your computer (eg OnyX xxx for macOS Catalina 10:15). When the download is complete, open the OnyX.dmg file obtained, click on the Accept button and drag the OnyX icon to the Applications folder of the system.

At this point, go to the folder in question, right-click on the OnyX icon and click on the Open item. Now, do what is indicated in the window that opened on the screen. Go to System Preferences (the gray icon with the gears in the Dock bar or Launchpad), click on the item Security and Privacy, select the Privacy tab located at the top right and click on the padlock symbol located at the bottom left .

Then type the password of your user account on Mac (the one you use to log in to the system) and click the Unlock button. Then select the item Full access to the disk from the sidebar located on the left, affix the check mark on the OnyX box and consent to restart the application, by clicking on the Exit button that appears on the screen.

Click, therefore, on the OK button in the box with the suggestions that had opened on the screen, so as to close it, and then reopen OnyX from the Launchpad. Now, type the Mac administration password in the appropriate text field, click the OK button and you're done.

Now, select the Utility tab of OnyX, went to the Scripts section, put the check mark next to the items Daily script, Weekly script and Monthly script and click Run to start the execution of the cron scripts, the maintenance scripts that are used to keep system performance stable (they are performed automatically by the system but occasionally it is good to "force" them). If you are asked to close all running programs and / or restart your computer to apply the changes, accept.

Then move to the Maintenance section, check the System checkbox (it is actually checked by default) and click the Options button to access the advanced settings. In the window that opens, then, make sure that the boxes relating to the cache files you wish to remove with OnyX (eg Kernel Cache and Extensions, Component Cache, etc.) are ticked and then click on the OK button.

Check the disk status

Previous versions of the Apple operating system for Mac, namely OS X, include a convenient application, called Disk Utility, which allows you to check for logical errors on the disk and repairs users' access to files and applications. Carrying out both these operations - if there are many errors on the disk - can improve the general performance of the Mac.

To correct the errors on the computer's startup disk (the one on which the operating system is installed) you must reboot the system and access the Mac recovery mode by holding down the cmd + r keys on the keyboard during power-up. Next, you need to set the language usage, start Disk Utility and select the Mac boot disk icon from the left sidebar. Finally, you must press the Repair disk permissions button, wait for the procedure to be completed and proceed to repair the disk by clicking on the appropriate button. Both procedures should take a few minutes.

Reset PRAM

Have you ever heard of PRAM? No? Then I'll quickly explain what it is. PRAM (also known as NVRAM on computers other than Macs) is a small non-volatile memory in which information such as screen resolution, boot disk address and speaker volume is stored.

Following hardware changes or the use of particular software, the information it holds can be altered in such a way as to cause small system slowdowns.
The procedure must be performed with the Mac turned off, so the first step you need to take is to completely shut down the computer by clicking on the apple icon in the menu bar and selecting the Turn off ... item from the menu that appears.
At this point, turn the Mac back on, simultaneously press the cmd + alt + P + R keys and hold them down until you hear the second boot "gong".
Now release the keys and wait for macOS (or earlier versions) to start to find out if the malfunctions you previously warned have disappeared.
If you notice an unusual slowness in starting the system, do not worry, it is normal after resetting the PRAM.

Turn off animations and transparencies

If you want to speed up Mac because you experience fluidity problems in the operating system animations (e.g. when switching from one desk to another or in the display of Mission Control), try disabling the multiple graphic options present in macOS (or previous versions).

To disable transparency effects (only on OS X Yosemite) - Go to System Preferences, click on Accessibility and select Monitor and then tick the Reduce transparency option.

To turn off transparency effects and increase color contrast (only on OS X Yosemite, it has a greater effect on speeding up animations) - Go to System Preferences, click on Accessibility, click on Monitor and put the check on the option Increase contrast.

To disable animations in the Dock bar - Go to System Preferences, click Dock and uncheck the Magnification and Animation options when opening applications.
To disable other system animations (such as opening new ones and scrolling the Web pages) - Open the OnyX application I already told you about in the previous lines, went to the Parameters tab, click on General and remove the tick the option Activate effect when opening windows.

Free up disk space

Contrary to what is often read around, there is no close relationship between system performance and available disk space. Having plenty of free disk space increases system performance when there is not enough RAM and some data that should be in the latter is moved to the hard disk (when the so-called swap occurs), but otherwise deleting files will not will help speed up your Mac.

In any case, I recommend you try Daisy Disk, a very practical application that analyzes the Mac disk and indicates where the bulky files are located. It costs EUR 9.99 but there is also a free version that does not automatically delete the files (it leaves the user the task of doing the "cleaning").

Alternatively, and if macOS Sierra is installed on your Mac, you can use the new tool for managing the data stored on your computer. You can access it immediately by clicking on the apple-shaped button located at the top left of the menu bar, clicking on About this Mac, selecting the Archive tab and then

clicking on the Manage ... button that you find next to the icon.
hard drive of your Mac.

Once the tool screen is displayed, you can choose whether or
not to perform specific operations (e.g. optimize storage on
iTunes, automatically empty the trash and so on) attached to
the Recommendations tab by simply pressing the relevant
button. For a more targeted operation, click on the various
Applications, Recycle Bin, Documents, Photos, iCloud Drive,
Mail and System tabs located on the left side and evaluate
whether to perform or, based on what your needs are, the
proposed operations .

Hardware upgrades

If the available space on the disk does not substantially affect
the performance of the system, an SSD instead of a mechanical
disk and a greater amount of RAM do it all right.
This means that one of the best ways to speed up a computer
(not just Macs) is to replace the hard disk with a solid state
drive (SSD) and RAM with a larger capacity memory.

Unfortunately, both of these operations cannot be performed
on MacBook Pro Retina (including the latest models) and
MacBook Air which have all the components welded inside.
If you have a MacBook Pro (not Retina) or an iMac, however,
there are no problems. You can upgrade your computer in a
very simple way by purchasing RAM and SSD drive to be
installed manually (or through a technician, if you do not feel
like doing everything yourself).

Install and manage antivirus (Windows \ Mac)

In the Mac world, antivirus is not essential. They are beginning to be useful - yes - but they still do not have a fundamental importance as on Windows computers.
How come I tell you about it? Simple, because some antivirus for Mac are not yet perfect and lead to noticeable system slowdowns. If you installed one recently, he may be the culprit for your computer's slowness!

If you want some advice, try uninstalling it and see if the situation improves. If successful, if your Mac returns to work quickly after removing the antivirus, consider what to do.

If you are aware of not taking particular risks, not frequent "dangerous" sites and do not exchange files with Windows systems (which could become infected with viruses transmitted by your computer, which however would be immune to them) you could avoid installing other antivirus.

Preliminary operations

Before looking for an antivirus / antimalware to be installed on your Mac, put these little common sense tips into practice and you will already be halfway done.

Verify that Gatekeeper is active. Gatekeeper is a feature included in all the latest versions of macOS (from Mountain Lion onwards) that strengthens the malware controls present in the Apple operating system by preventing the execution of apps from non-certified developers. To verify the correct functioning of this function on your Mac, open System Preferences (the gear icon located in the Dock bar), move to Security and Privacy and make sure that in the General tab of the window that opens there is the check mark next to App Store and identified developers. If the option in question is not selected, click on the lock icon located at the bottom left, type the password of your user account on macOS, press Enter and select it.

Do not install applications from unreliable sources. Install only the applications found on the Mac App Store and those from reliable developers (eg Adobe, Microsoft, Google etc.). Avoid pirated software in the most absolute way (not only because they are dangerous, but also because they are illegal) and if possible avoid the use of plugins such as Java or Flash Player which are more and more often the vehicle of cyber attacks.

Use Mac antimalware. The reason why we are here today. To sleep relatively peacefully, install good antimalware software on your Mac and use it occasionally to check the system status. A solution for on-demand scanning should suffice, but if you use the computer in a professional context and / or are responsible for the security of others' data you could also consider more complete solutions with real-time control. Now let's avoid further ado and see which Mac antivirus to use.

Malwarebytes Anti-Malware (free)

Viruses are a specific type of malware (i.e. malicious software) designed to alter / damage the data on the infected computer, replicate and propagate the infection on other machines. On Mac there are relatively few of them but there are other types of malware, often less "destructive" than viruses but still dangerous, which you must learn to deal with.

One of the best solutions that currently allow you to deal with malware on Mac is Malwarebytes Anti-Malware, Mac version of one of the best antimalware available for Windows. With Malwarebytes for macOS it is possible to remove malware and adware (unwanted software that displays advertising content during Internet browsing and / or daily use of the computer) in on-demad mode without weighing down the system and without the slightest effort. Just start the software, click on a button and you're done.

A paid version of Malwarebytes Anti-Malware is also available, which costs 39.99 euros / year and also includes the real-time protection module, but at the moment I don't consider it necessary for what your needs are.

To download the free version of Malwarebytes Anti-Malware on your Mac, therefore connected to the official website of the program and click on the Free Download button located in the center of the page. When the download is complete, open the Malwarebytes pkg package and, in the window that appears on the screen, first click on the Continue button three times in succession and then on Accept and Install. Type, then, the administration password of the Mac, from Enter, wait for the end of the installation of the program and click first on Close and then on Move to finish the setup.

At this point, start Malwarebytes Anti-Malware, press the Scan now button and wait for the system scan to be completed (it will take a few minutes). If suspicious items emerge from the check, make sure there is a check mark next to their names and click on the button to remove them (if necessary, also accept the system restart). If, however, no threat is detected, close the program window directly.

Bitdefender (free / paid)

Bitdefender is one of the few antivirus products that have been promoted with flying colors in the AV-Test.org comparative tests, has a threat detection rate of 100% and does not weigh down the system. It is available in two versions: a free one that only performs on-demand scans and a paid one (39.99 euros / year) which instead includes a module for real-time protection. In both versions, it can recognize both macOS and Windows malware, so it is also useful for those looking for only an antivirus to check the files to be shared with friends' PCs.

The free version of Bitdefender, called Virus Scanner, you can download it directly from the Mac App Store while the paid version you have to download from the official website of the application by clicking on the item TRY NOW A 30-DAY TRIAL VERSION, creating a free account on the site Bitdefender and pressing first on INSTALL BITDEFENDER and then on DOWNLOAD. To install the software on your Mac, open the Bitdefender_xx.pkg file that you have downloaded to your computer and always click Continue / Accept.

You will be able to use the product for free for 30 days before purchasing it. If the installation package does not start and an error message appears, right-click on its icon and select the Open item from the menu that appears.

Bitdefender operation is extremely intuitive in both versions of the software. To use the free edition of the antivirus, for example, just update the definitions by clicking on the Update now button and start a complete system scan by pressing on Deep System Scan. If you want to scan only the critical areas of the system (those where malware is most commonly hidden) or you want to check a specific folder, use the Scan Critical Locations and Scan a Custom location buttons.

AVG (Free)

AVG Free is another of the few antiviruses that managed to achieve 100% effectiveness in the comparative tests of AV-Test.org. It has real-time protection, it slows down the system a little more than Bitdefender (the one paid for with the real-time protection module) but this should not be a problem, the Mac's performance should still remain at excellent levels.

To download AVG Free to your computer, connected to the application's website and click first on the Free download button and then on Download Now. Once the download is complete, open the dmg package that you have taken from the AVG website and start the executable Install AVG Antivirus contained within it.

In the window that opens, first click on Continue two consecutive times and then on Accept and Install. Then type the password of your user account on macOS, press the Enter key on the computer keyboard and conclude the setup by clicking first on Close.
At this point, the initial configuration of AVG should start. Then click on the Continue button, create your free account on the AVG network to activate your copy of the software (just type an email address and password in the appropriate text fields and press the Create account button) and click on the Go to dashboard button to access the main antivirus screen.

Now you are free to start a full system scan by pressing the Scan Mac button, or to scan individual files by dragging them into the appropriate box. To activate or deactivate real-time system protection, use the lever located under Realtime protection.

Note: if you decide to uninstall AVG, do not drag the trash application icon. Start the software, click on the AVG AntiVirus menu located at the top left and select the Uninstall AVG AntiVirus item from the latter. In the window that opens, then click on the Continue button, type the password of your user account on macOS, press Enter, click on Finish and you're done.

Set up system recovery

If you want to format Windows 10 using the Reset PC function, the first thing you need to do is to access the Windows Update and Security section. To do this, type in the search field attached to the taskbar the term settings, click on the first result attached to the list that is shown to you in the Start menu and then presses on the item Update and security present in the new window that went to open on the desktop.

Now on the Restore item located in the sidebar on the left then click on the button To start which is in the Reset your PC section.

Now choose the Keep my files option, if it is your intention to format Windows 10 by going to remove the apps and settings but continuing to keep your personal files (photos, text documents, etc.), or choose the Remove option everything, if you want to remove anything that is stored on your computer.

On some PCs, generally laptops, you can also find the option Restore default settings that allows you to restore the computer to its factory state, i.e. with the same programs, services etc. that you had found on the same at the time of purchase.

At this point, if you have selected the option Keep my files, follow the appropriate wizard visible on the screen by always pressing the Next button and waiting for the formatting of the operating system to be started and completed. In case of second thoughts, press the Cancel button.

If, on the other hand, you have chosen the Remove all option, indicate in the window that you are then shown on the screen if you only want to remove your personal files or if you also want to clean the drive. In the first case, press on Remove only my personal files while in the second case click on Remove files and clean the drive.

Keep in mind that the first option allows you to format Windows 10 faster but is less secure while the second option may take up to a few hours but will make it extremely difficult for third parties to recover files. In both cases, then stick to the appropriate wizard that is shown on the screen. In case of second thoughts, press the Cancel button.

The computer will then restart and start the initial Windows 10 configuration procedure during which you can adjust various operating system settings. If you prefer to speed things up, you can click Use Quick Settings to use the default settings. Then proceed to associate your Microsoft account with Windows or create a local account to be able to immediately resume using your PC with Windows 10 installed.

Once completed the procedure by which to format Windows 10, do not forget to activate your copy of the operating system by providing the product key of the same in your possession again. To do this, access the Settings section of the operating system, click Activation and then select the option on the right to provide your product key and to activate your copy of Windows 10. When the procedure is completed you will see the entry Windows is activated in the Activation field.

Mac \ MacOS Recovery

macOS Recovery makes it easy to reinstall the Mac operating system, even when you first need to initialize the boot disk. All you need is an internet connection. If a wireless network is available, you can choose it from the Wi-Fi menu in the menu bar. This menu is also available in macOS Recovery.

1. Boot from macOS Recovery

To boot from macOS Recovery, turn on your Mac and immediately press one of the following key combinations, holding it down. Release the keys when an Apple logo, a spinning globe, or another startup screen appears.

Command (⌘) -R

Reinstall the latest version of macOS previously installed on the Mac (recommended).

Option-⌘-R

Upgrade to the latest version of macOS compatible with the Mac.

Shift-Option-⌘-R

Reinstall the version of macOS that came with your Mac or the closest version still available.

You may be asked to enter a password, such as the firmware password or the password of a user who is an administrator of the Mac. Enter the password required to continue.

When the Utility window appears, it means that you have completed booting from macOS Recovery.

2. Decide whether to initialize (format) the disk

Initialization will probably not be necessary unless you intend to sell, swap or sell your Mac or in case of problems that require initialization. If you need to initialize before installing macOS, select Disk Utility in the Utility window, then click Continue.

3. Install macOS

When you decide to reinstall macOS, choose Reinstall macOS from the Utility window, then click Continue and follow the instructions on the screen. You will be asked to choose a disk on which to install.

If the installer asks to unlock the disc, enter the password you use to log in to the Mac.

If the installer does not detect the disk or a message indicates that the installation cannot be performed on the computer or volume, you may need to initialize the disk before proceeding.

For the installation to complete, do not put your Mac to sleep or close the lid. During installation, your Mac may restart, a progress bar may appear multiple times, and the screen may sometimes appear blank for a few minutes.

If the setup assistant appears on reboot, but you're about to sell, swap or give away your Mac, press Command-Q to exit Setup Assistant without completing the procedure. Finally, click Turn Off. When the new owner starts the Mac, they can use their data to complete the setting.

MacOS Recovery exceptions

The version of macOS offered by macOS Recovery may, in certain circumstances, be different:

If you have never installed macOS Sierra 10.12.4 or later on your Mac, Option-Command-R installs the version of macOS that came with your Mac or the closest version still available. The Shift-Option-Command-R combination is not available.

If you initialized the entire disk instead of just the boot volume on the disk, macOS Recovery may offer only the version of macOS that came with your Mac or the closest version still available. You can upgrade to a later version later.

If your Mac has the Apple T2 security chip and you have never installed a macOS update, Option-Command-R installs the latest version of macOS installed on the Mac.

If the Mac logic board has just been replaced as part of a repair, macOS Recovery may only offer the latest version of macOS compatible with the Mac.

How to forcefully close a program

Windows

To close a program that has crashed and is unable to close normally, press the following key combination on the keyboard: CTRL + ALT + DEL.

At this point click "start task management", that is the task manager, go to the "Processes" tab and look for the process corresponding to the blocked software. Very often the process is called as the program (plus the .exe extension), once you have identified the process select it and click on "End Process". In this way the program will be forced to close.

Mac

As for macOS, on the other hand, you have two ways of forcibly quitting blocked programs: the first involves the use of the Force Quit Applications utility and allows you to stop applications that no longer respond immediately.

To use it, press the key combination cmd + alt + esc on the Mac keyboard (it should work even when the system seems blocked), choose the program that no longer responds - which should be marked by a specific indication - from the window proposed to screen and, to stop it, double click on the Forced Exit button.

The changes on any open files in the program just closed will not be saved.
Alternatively, if the system is extremely slow but not completely blocked, you can get a more complete list of the processes active on the computer (and not just the open programs) by using the Activity Monitor utility, which you can call from the Launchpad's Other folder (the rocket icon attached to the Dock bar).

Once the program has started, which is extremely similar to Windows Task Manager, click on the CPU tab and then on the% CPU column to find out which processes are using the processor the most; in the same way, go to the Memory tab and click on the Memory column to find the processes that require more RAM.

Once the process has been identified, you can end it by selecting its name and clicking first on the [X] located at the top left and then on the Forced exit button.

Eliminate virus from pc

Are you worried that your computer has been infected with a virus but the antivirus you are currently using doesn't detect anything suspicious? If I were you I would try to use another software or even, if the situation requires it, to download one of those antiviruses that copy themselves on external media (CDs or USB sticks) and run outside the operating system. I know, it's a bit boring to do, but when your privacy and the security of your data are at stake, it is better to be cautious. Courage then! Take a few minutes of free time and find out with me how to eliminate viruses from your PC using the best cybersecurity solutions currently available for free.

To effectively protect your PC and fight computer viruses, even the most fearsome ones, there is no need to buy expensive commercial suites. There are excellent antiviruses even among zero-cost software, and today I will report the most reliable ones, that is, those that in the comparative tests have obtained the best results. Come on, let's do it!

Traditional antivirus

This is a so-called "traditional" antivirus: the one to be installed and kept constantly active on the computer to prevent, and eliminate, the infections caused by computer viruses. Here is one of the best

Avira Free Antivirus has a level of effectiveness practically equal to that of Bitdefender.

According to the latest comparative tests, it is slightly "heavier" than the latter, but we are talking about almost imperceptible differences. The only real flaw is that it does not preventively check the contents of e-mail, a function reserved for the paid version of the software.

To download the free version of Avira on your computer, connected to its official website and click on the Free download button. When the download is complete, open the installation package called avira_it_av_xx__ws.exe and click first on Accept and install and then on Yes.

Once this is done, the download and subsequent installation of the actual antivirus will start. You can track the progress of the procedure by clicking on the red umbrella icon located in the notification area, near the Windows clock. The procedure, I warn you right away, could go on for a few minutes given that considering that approximately 130 MB of data will have to be downloaded from the Internet, it all depends on the speed of your Internet connection.

In addition, during the antivirus download phase you will be offered to download some additional software developed by Avira: Phantom VPN to browse securely via a VPN; Avira System Speedup to optimize the PC; the SafeSearch Plus browser add-on and Avira Software Updater to download updates for programs installed on your PC. I advise you to leave them all alone, and then close the installation window by clicking on the "x" button located at the top right.

Once the download is complete, immediately start a complete system check by clicking on the Avira icon in the notification area of the PC and selecting the Free antivirus item from the menu that appears. Then, select the System scanner item from the left sidebar, click on Local drives, press the button with the magnifying glass and the Windows flag and wait for the result of the scan to be provided to you.
If you need, you can also start scanning individual files. To do this, just right-click on them and choose the appropriate item from the contextual menu that is shown to you.

Mac

If your problems mainly concern Web browsing and, for example, you are redirected to sites full of advertisements, try to check the list of extensions in the browser and remove the ones you suspect. Below you will find all the steps to be taken on the most popular browsers.

Safari - if you use Safari (the default macOS browser), you can check the list of extensions installed in it by going to the

Safari> Preferences menu (top left) and selecting the Extensions tab from the window that opens. At this point, locate the suspicious extension from the left sidebar and remove it, by clicking first on its name and then on the Uninstall button that appears on the right (then confirming the operation).

Chrome - if you use Chrome, can you check the list of extensions installed in the browser by clicking on the button? (top right) and selecting the items Other tools> Extensions from the menu that appears. In the new tab that opens in the browser, locate the extension you want to delete and click first on the trash can icon located next to it and then on the Remove button.

Firefox - in Firefox, you can check the list of extensions installed in the browser by clicking on the button? located at the top right and going to Add-ons (in the menu that appears). In the tab that opens, then select the Extensions item from the left sidebar, locate the add-on to be removed and click on the Remove button located in front of its name.

Enable macOS protections

The Mac operating system, macOS, includes several features that prevent and counter malware infections. The best known is called Gatekeeper and is the one that prevents the execution of software that come from non-certified developers. By keeping the Gatekeeper function active (which is available in macOS Lion 10.7.5 and later), the Mac does not run the programs that are downloaded outside the Mac App Store and that are not attributable to certified developers, therefore of proven reliability: this prevents you from running potentially dangerous software and, therefore, from being affected by malware.

To verify that the Gatekeeper function is active and correctly configured on your Mac, open System Preferences (the gear icon located on the Dock bar), go to Security and Privacy and select the General tab from the window that opens.

At this point, if you see that next to the App Store and identified developers item there is a check mark, do nothing: Gatekeeper is already configured correctly. Otherwise, click on the padlock icon located at the bottom left, type the password of your user account on macOS (the one you use to access the system) and enter, then put the check mark next to the App Store item and identified developers and you're done.

The App Store option is also available, which would make the Mac even safer, but I consider it too limited as it only allows programs downloaded from the Mac App Store to run. If you want more info on Gatekeeper and its operation, consult the official Apple website.

Another security feature included in macOS, less known, is Xprotect: a real antimalware, complete with signature database, which Apple silently updates over time and which automatically blocks the execution of malicious software. It is enabled by default, but its updates - which are critical for effective system protection - may be disabled.

To check whether updates for Xprotect are enabled, open System Preferences, go to the App Store and make sure there is a check mark next to the item Install system data files and security updates. Otherwise, click on the padlock icon located at the bottom left, type the password of your user account on macOS (the one you use to access the system) and enter. At this point, put the check mark next to the item Install system data files and security updates and you're done.

Once you have activated the security measures in macOS and downloaded a good antimalware (to be used from time to time to control the computer), you should be able to sleep relatively peacefully. In any case, don't believe you are "invincible". If you download software from unreliable sites and bypass macOS restrictions (accepting their execution despite system warnings) you could still attract malware.

My advice, therefore, is to download programs from reliable sources (primarily the Mac App Store) and absolutely avoid software from the BitTorrent network or from file hosting services (which are very often also illegal). Bypass Gatekeeper restrictions only with proven software, such as LibreOffice, which is not from Apple certified developers but is absolutely safe as a program.

How to uninstall a software

Windows

Wandering around your system, did you just realize that there are still useless software installed on the hard disk a long time ago and do you want to delete them?

Well, let's get started, let's take a brief review of the standard program removal procedure from the Microsoft operating system.

If you use a version of Windows equal to or later than Vista, you can uninstall a program from your PC by going to Control Panel, selecting the item Uninstall a program from the latter and clicking first on the name of the software to be deleted and then on the Uninstall / Change that is at the top. At this point, the wizard for uninstalling the selected software should start, which usually consists of always clicking on the Next (or Next) button.

If you use Windows 10 you can also follow another procedure: you can uninstall a program from your computer by clicking on the Start button (the flag icon located in the lower left corner of the screen), selecting the gear icon from the menu which opens and going first to the System and then to the App and functionality. At this point, select the name of the application to be removed, press twice on the Uninstall button and complete the wizard for deleting the software by always clicking on Next or Next.

Mac

As I said previously, the procedure to uninstall a Mac program is not the same in all cases, although usually it is sufficient to take advantage of the tools included in the operating system. Below, I will explain step by step, how to proceed using the Launchpad, the Trash, the tool to manage the storage space included in macOS and the official unistallers distributed by the various software houses.

Via the Launchpad

Let's start by discovering how to uninstall a program from Mac via the Launchpad, a procedure that applies only and exclusively to applications that have been downloaded and installed via the Mac App Store.

Now all you have to do is access the macOS Launchpad by clicking on its icon (the one with the space rocket and the gray background) that you find on the Dock bar and locate, in the screen that is shown to you, the application icon in which you are interested in going to act (if you cannot see it, scroll through the subsequent screens of the Launchpad by clicking on the dots located at the bottom or swiping on the trackpad).

Once you find the application you want to delete, make a long click on it, until the icon starts to "shake". Next, click on the "x" that appears in the upper right corner of the icon, then on the Delete button, and you're done.

Through the Bin

Another system to uninstall a program from Mac, valid for applications installed via the .dmg package and dragging it to the Applications folder, consists in dragging the software to the MacOS Bin, proceeding in a practically analogous way to what needs to be done to delete a file .

So to get rid of an application on Mac in this way, first of all, go to the Applications folder of your computer. If you do not know how to find it, go to the desk, open the Go menu located in the upper left part of the screen and select the Applications item from the latter. Alternatively, you can press the key combination cmd + shift + a on the computer keyboard or you can select the Applications link from the Finder sidebar.

Once you reach the previous folder, locate the icon of the software to be uninstalled, make a long click on it and, continuing to keep clicked, drag the latter to the Trash, which is located in the bottom right part of the Dock bar.

After completing all these steps, you may be asked to type the password of your user account on macOS (the one you use to enter the system) and you will then have to empty the Trash: to do this, click with the right mouse button on the the icon of the latter, select the item Empty the Trash from the menu that appears and confirm everything by clicking on the Empty the bin button.

Using the tool to manage the storage space

An additional system that you have available to uninstall the applications installed on the Mac is to take advantage of the tool to manage the storage space, the one that Apple has decided to include on its operating system starting from macOS Sierra. You can use it both to delete applications from the Mac App Store and from external sources.

To use it, click on the apple icon located at the top left of the screen and select, from the menu that opens, the item About this Mac. In the window that is shown on your desktop, select the Storage tab and then click on the Manage button, which you will find next to the name of your computer's hard drive.
In the further window that is now shown to you, select the Applications item from the left sidebar, identify the application you wish to delete, select it and press the Delete button, located at the bottom, to proceed with its cancellation. Then confirm what your intentions are, by clicking again on the Delete button in the box that appears, and you're done.

In some circumstances, programs uninstalled from the Mac can leave unwanted traces on the computer, a bit like Windows does. To prevent this from happening, then to go to completely uninstall a program from the Mac, you can use special third-party removal tools.

AppCleaner

The best tool available on the market to uninstall the programs installed on the Mac without leaving residual files is the free AppCleaner software that acts by analyzing the contents of the disk and removing the selected programs so that they do not leave data in the system.
To download AppCleaner on your Mac, connect to the Internet site of the program www.freemacsoft.net/appcleaner/. click on the first Version x.x link located in the right sidebar, under the heading Downloads.

Once the download is complete, extract the ZIP archive obtained and drag the AppCleaner icon (the one with the program logo) inside it

into the macOS Applications folder. Next, right-click on it and select the Open item from the menu that appears, in order to start the application, however, going around the limitations imposed by Apple towards uncertified developers (an operation that must be done only at the first start).
Now that you see the AppCleaner window on your desktop, drag the icon of the software you want to uninstall over it and click the Remove button. When prompted, type in your user account password on macOS and you're done.

Alternatively, you can also click on the button with the horizontal lines located in the upper right part of the window, so as to view the complete list of installed applications directly from AppCleaner, and identify the one you want to remove from the latter.

Once you find the program you want to uninstall, click on its name and then on the Remove button in the box that opens. In some cases, you may also be asked to type the password of your user account on Mac, to confirm the operation. In the program preferences you can also remove the protections for running programs and system ones (although, in general, I do not recommend you adopt this solution).

The same procedure just described for the applications can also be put into practice for the widgets and plugins installed in the system, by first selecting the reference category from the drop-down menu located at the top of the AppCleaner window, visible after clicking on the button with horizontal lines.

Install a browser

example Chrome Windows

Your friends suggested that you replace the default web browser on your computer with Google Chrome to navigate faster on the Internet but, as you are not very skilled in the technological field, you don't know how to download and install this program? No problem, I'll help you. Take a few minutes of free time and concentrate on reading this guide entirely dedicated to how to install Google Chrome and you will see that in the end you will have much clearer ideas on what to do.

Before giving all the necessary explanations, I want to explain the nature of this browser. Chrome is a free navigation program developed by Google. It is compatible with all major operating systems: Windows, macOS, Linux, Android and iOS and among its main strengths are an amazing speed in opening web pages, support for many extensions that allow you to expand its functionality and automatic synchronization of data (history, extensions, favorites, etc.) on all devices. It includes the Adobe Flash Player "as standard" and updates itself completely automatically without the user having to do anything.

In short, it must be tried. Also because it coexists without problems with Internet Explorer, Firefox, Safari and Opera and allows you to import bookmarks and preferences from other browsers with a simple click. Then? Can you know what you're still doing there?

If you want to install Google Chrome on a Windows PC, the first step you need to take is to connect to the program's website using

Internet Explorer and press the Download Chrome button in the center of the screen. If you prefer to avoid that usage statistics and reports on browser crashes are subsequently sent, remove the check mark from the box that refers to the relative option attached to the box shown on the screen, then click on Accept and Install to accept the terms of service of the browser and then on Yes to start the download procedure.

If you have not used Internet Explorer to download Chrome, after clicking on Accept and install you must consent to saving the installation file of the program, wait for it to be downloaded and launch it. The software will take care of the rest.

Within a few seconds you will see the Chrome welcome screen and you can start "surfing" the Web by typing the addresses of the sites to visit in the bar located at the top or by searching (always from the latter).
To import bookmarks, search engines and passwords from Internet Explorer or other browsers, click on the Import bookmarks item now located on the Chrome homepage (top left). To activate the synchronization of browsing data on multiple devices, however, click on the little man icon located in the title bar (top right) and log in with your Google account.

Chrome for Mac

Would you like to understand how to download Chrome on macOS? So, to begin with, open the browser you currently use to surf the Internet on your Mac (eg Safari), then go to the main page of the site dedicated to the "big G" browser.

At this point, click on the Download Chrome button in the center of the page displayed and, in the box that you see appear on the screen, click on the Accept and install button.
Then, open the googlechrome.dmg package obtained and, through the window that opens, drag the Chrome icon to the macOS Applications folder. Then, open the latter, right click on the browser icon and select the Open item twice in a row, in order to start Chrome, however, going around the limitations wanted by Apple

towards third-party developers (an operation that should only be done at first start).

To conclude, choose, via the screen that opens on the desktop, whether to set Chrome as the default browser and whether to send anonymous usage statistics and reports on anonymous stops to Google, leaving or removing the check from the appropriate boxes, then click on the button Launch Google Chrome and you will finally find yourself in front of the main browser window.

Keep in mind that if you want to sync extensions, favorites and other data with all the devices you use Chrome on, you can do it by clicking on the little man icon in the upper right part of the browser window and pressing the button to sign in to your Google Account.

Transfer files from PC to USB drive

Windows

To transfer files from a Windows PC to a USB drive, you can use some methods that require the use of the predefined tools of this operating system.
The first solution you can use is File Explorer, the default file manager of the Microsoft operating system. Now connect the stick to

the computer's USB port and start File Explorer, through its icon in the system tray (or press the Windows + E key combination).

In the screen that is shown to you, click on the wording This PC, which you find in the left sidebar, and find the USB flash drive icon among those available in the Devices and drives section.

Now, reach the folder where the files you need to transfer are located, opening another File Explorer window using the method I indicated in the previous lines or, if the folder is present on the desktop, by double-clicking on it.
Now select the files to be transferred by holding down the Ctrl key on the keyboard and left-clicking on each one. If you want to select them all, press the key combination Ctrl + A. Now that you have highlighted the files, right-click on one of them and, in the contextual menu that is shown to you, select the Copy item, in case you want to keep a copy of the data on your computer, or the one called Cut , in case you want to completely move it.

If you want to transfer the entire folder containing the files, right-click on it and, in the menu that opens, select the Copy or Cut items. At this point, go back to the section of Windows File Explorer that you opened before, relating to the main root of the USB drive. Click with the right mouse button on any empty point inside the window and, in the context menu, select the Paste item. Doing so will begin the process of transferring files from your computer to the USB drive.

As an alternative to the above method, I can point you to another quick solution for transferring data to the USB drive. After inserting it into the USB port of the computer, go to the folder where the files to be transferred are located and right-click on it to show you a context menu.

In case you want to transfer only specific files, access the folder and follow the procedure I indicated in the previous lines, in order to highlight only the files to be moved.
Whether you want to transfer the folder or just some files, after right-clicking on them, in the context menu select the Send to>

[USB stick name] items, to start transferring data to the main root of the USB device .
After the transfer is complete, it's time to remove the computer's USB stick. Then click on the icon with the ^ symbol that you find in the taskbar at the bottom right, near the clock.

In the screen that is shown to you, press the icon with the symbol of a USB flash drive and, in the contextual menu, choose the Eject [name of USB flash drive] item. You will be shown a message to indicate that you can now safely remove the USB drive from your PC.

Use external storage devices with your Mac

External hard drives, sticks, USB drives, flash memory cards, and devices like iPods are examples of storage devices that you can connect to your Mac using Thunderbolt, USB or FireWire cables, or by connecting wirelessly using Bluetooth.

Storage devices (such as external hard drives) may also be available on the network. In addition, you can insert flash memory cards from your camera or other device into the SDXC card slot on Mac. If your Mac does not have a card slot, you can access data on the flash memory card using a connected card reader.

After connecting the storage device, you can move the files from the Mac to the storage device or vice versa.

Connect a storage device

Connect your device to your Mac using the cable that came with it, then use the Finder to view the connected device. If the cable does not have a connector suitable for Mac, you may need to use an adapter. Consult the documentation supplied with the device.

Move files to or from an external storage device

Make sure your Mac is connected to your external storage device (for example, using a USB cable or via a network).

Click the Finder icon in the Dock to open a Finder window, then do one of the following to move the files.

Move files to a storage device: select one or more files on the desktop or in a folder, then drag them to the storage device, available under Locations in the sidebar of the Finder.

Move files from a storage device: Select the storage device, listed under Locations in the sidebar of the Finder, then drag the files you want to place on the Mac.

If you don't have permission to view or work with files on a storage device

If you are not the administrator of the Mac, ask the administrator to give you access to the files you need.

If you are the administrator of the Mac, do one of the following.

Authenticate as an administrator user: Depending on the method you use to try to access the file, you may be asked to authenticate as an administrator user.

Change the "Sharing and Permissions" settings for the file: For instructions, see Use file sharing.

Eject a storage device (USB drive, flash drive or other device)

On the Mac, do one of the following:

Select the item you want to eject, then choose File> Eject.

In the Finder sidebar, click the Eject button next to the item name.

On the desk, drag the item you want to eject into the Trash.
If you are unable to eject a storage device, another app or another user may currently be using one or more files located on the storage device.

How to search files inside the pc (Windows)

Congratulations, once again you managed to lose a written text document no more than a few minutes ago. How do you say? Is this just a coincidence and are you able to find all your important documents in the blink of an eye? Well, then I'll test you! Tell me: in which folder did you save the latest programs downloaded from the Internet? Where are your photos, videos and music? Come on, tell me ... tick, tick, time is running out ... I knew it, you don't remember it: your computer is always in a mess and you always take a long time to look for a file.

I also bet that to track down the files you need, manually browse the folders on your computer in search of lost documents and that this makes you waste a lot of time. It's so true? Well, it's not exactly wrong, but there are simpler and faster methods, both on Windows and Mac computers. Have you ever heard of the Windows search bar? What about Spotlight Search? Did you know that you can also download a free program on your computer that allows you to search for files at the speed of light?
If the answer to these questions is negative, then this is the tutorial for you. I'll tell you how to use some indispensable tools to search for files on your computer. Are you ready to start? All you need is a few minutes of free time: sit comfortably because I'm about to start with the step-by-step explanation. I wish you a good read.

The files on your computer are automatically indexed so that they can be easily found through the Windows Search function. Before tackling how to search through this Windows tool, you will need to check whether the Indexing Options are set correctly according to your needs.

Then click on the button on the bottom left (Search) with a magnifying glass icon. Then type the wording indexing options and select the result corresponding to your search. When you're done, the Windows Indexing Options panel will open. In the central section, you can see which items are indexed and, therefore, where to search for what you type in Windows. If you want to add a new search path, click on the Edit button to open a new window. Then put a check mark on the boxes relating to the paths you want to add and click Ok. Then click the Close button.

Your computer will index the files and, in the case of text documents, also their content.
To perform a search, simply click on the Windows Search button (icon with a magnifying glass symbol) located at the bottom left, and type the full name (or part of it) of the file. The results will be shown on the screen and you can select one of the search terms that are shown to you, if they correspond to what you have typed and are looking for.

If, on the other hand, you have to search for a file that is located in a folder, simply type in the name of the entire file (or part of it) in the Search box found at the top right of the Explorer window of the folder you open . You will also be shown, within the folder, the list of files corresponding to your search. You can refine your searches by using the toolbar at the top in Windows File Explorer.

How to search for a file (macOS tools)

On macOS the procedure is just as simple. You can search for files on your Apple computer by clicking on the icon with the symbol of a magnifying glass that you see at the top right (Spotlight).

In the Spotlight Search field you will have to type the name of the file in full (or in part) in order for the search to start. You will then be shown on the screen all the results related to your search. Then select a file and double-click on it to open it.
Another method you can use to search on your Mac is to press the key combination Command + F (⌘ + F). A Finder window will open to perform a search within the macOS operating system. Then type in the Search field the name of the file you want to find.
If you want, you can refine your search by clicking on the [+] button, located at the top right, and selecting the two filters Type and Any.
Inside the Finder folder you will be shown the search results related to the term you typed.

How to set or change a password

Tired of having to type the same password every time?

If you are reading this tutorial right now it is clear that over time your needs have changed and now you like to know what you need to do to be able to put your password on your PC. How do you say? Is this the way it is? Well, then I'm happy to tell you that you can count on me.

In the following lines, in fact, I will illustrate all the various and possible steps that it is necessary to carry out in order to put the password on the PC. No, you won't have to do anything particularly complicated. Entering the password on the PC is in fact an operation as simple as removing it, you must trust.

So if you are interested in finding out what you need to do to be able to put your password on your PC, I suggest you take a few minutes of your free time to the indications that I am about to give you. I am sure that in the end you will succeed in your intent and that you will be able to tell you more than satisfied with it.

Before explaining what are the steps that need to be taken to put the password on the PC, there is one thing about which it is good to immediately clarify: the procedure that must be carried out is slightly different depending on the version of Windows installed on your computer. So find the version of Windows you use and stick to the relative indications.

Set the password on the PC - Windows 10

If you use Windows 10 and it is your intention to find out what you need to do to be able to put the password on your PC, you need to make some clarifications. If you have configured access on your computer via a Microsoft account, i.e. the same one you use to access all the other services of the company, probably what you want to do at this moment is to replace the typing of the password usually used by you with a PIN or with a graphic password. If instead you use a Microsoft account but this is not your case or if you use a local account then most likely in the past you have removed the Windows 10 access key and now you want to know how to proceed to put the password on the PC.

So if you use a Microsoft account and you are interested in finding out what you need to do to put the password on your PC by replacing the access key currently in use with a numeric PIN or with a graphic password the first thing you need to do is click on the appropriate field search located at the bottom right next to the Start button and type the term settings. Then select the Settings icon that appears in the search results.

Now select the Account item and then click Login Options from the left sidebar. Then press the Add button located under the wording PIN to configure a numeric PIN or the Add button located under the wording Graphic password to set a graphic password.
After carrying out the steps in question, the changes made will be applied immediately. This means that starting from the next access to the system, in order to log in you will have to type, according to the choice you made, the PIN or the graphic password.

If, on the other hand, you use a Microsoft account or a local account and you want to understand how to put the password on your PC, the first thing you need to do is to click on the search field located to the right of the Start button. Then type the term run and then press on the Run icon that appears among the search results. Now type the netplwiz command in the appropriate form attached to the Run window and then click the OK button.

In the new window select, using the left mouse button, your user account in the box located under the item Users for the computer: then put a check mark on the box located next to the item To use this computer the user must enter the name and password. Now click first on the Apply button located at the bottom and then also on the OK button in order to confirm and apply the changes.

Now type for the last time the password you intend to use on your Windows 10 PC by filling in the password fields: and confirm password: inherent to the new window displayed, then click OK.

Set the password on the PC - Windows 8 / Windows 8.1

Do you use a PC with Windows 8 or Windows 8.1 installed and want to understand what needs to be done to put the password? Yes? Well, then let's start by clarifying this point.

The basic concept is the same one that I already explained to you when I talked to you about how to put the password on the PC with Windows 10 installed. So, if on your computer you have configured access via a Microsoft account, probably what you want to do in this moment is to replace the typing of the password usually used by you with a PIN or with a graphic password. If instead you use a Microsoft account but this is not your case or if you use a local account then perhaps in the past you have removed the access key to Windows 8 or Windows 8.1 and now you want to know how to put the password on the PC.

So if you use a Microsoft account and you intend to understand how to put the password to the PC by taking advantage of a numeric PIN or a graphic password, first of all access the Start Screen then type the term pc settings using the appropriate search field located at the top right and then click on the PC Settings icon that is shown to you in the search results.

Proceed now going to select the Account item and then click Login Options from the left sidebar. Now presses the Add button located under the wording PIN to configure a numeric PIN or the Add button located under the wording Graphic password to set a graphic password. Then type in the password currently in use for your account and then click on the OK button and then fill in the fields displayed on the screen by entering the required information and confirm your willingness to make changes to how you access your account by pressing the Finish button.

After carrying out the following procedures, the changes made will be applied immediately.

Therefore, starting from the next access to the system, in order to log in you will have to type, based on the choice you made, the PIN or the graphic password.

If instead you use a Microsoft account or a local account and you want to understand what you need to do to put the password on your PC, the first thing you need to do is to access the Start Screen. Then click on the button depicting a magnifying glass which is located at the top right, type the term run in the search field displayed then click on the Run icon which is included in the search results. Now type the netplwiz command in the appropriate form attached to the Run window and then click the OK button.

In the new window that will be shown to you, select, using the left mouse button, your user account in the box located under the heading Users for the computer: then put a check mark on the box located next to the item To use this computer you must that the user enters the name and password. To confirm and apply the changes, first click on the Apply button located at the bottom and then also on the OK button.

To conclude, enter the password to be used on your Windows 8 or Windows 8.1 PC for the last time by filling in the password fields: and confirm password: listed in the new window that appears and then click OK.

Set the password on the PC - Windows 7

If you use Windows 7 and you want to be able to understand what you need to do to put the password on your PC, the first thing you need to do is press the Start button on the taskbar. Then click on the image relating to the user account in use present in the upper right part of the menu that went to open to immediately display the User Account section of the Control Panel.

In the new window on the desktop, click on the item Create a password for the account and then fill in the fields New password and Confirm new password by typing the access key that you intend to use in order to access your computer. Then fill in the Enter password hint field with a hint that allows you to easily remember the password you have chosen in case you have any difficulty then click on the Create password button to put the password on the PC.

After carrying out these procedures, the changes made will be applied immediately. Therefore, starting from the next access to the system, in order to log in you will have to type the chosen password.

Change the login password on the Mac

It is important to change your login password from time to time to protect privacy.
If you have forgotten your password, you need to reset it.

Note: the login password is the password you enter to unlock your Mac when you turn it on or wake it up from sleep. It is not the Apple ID password, which provides access to the iTunes Store, App Store, Apple Books, iCloud and other Apple services.

On the Mac, choose Apple menu> System Preferences, then click Users and Groups.
Click on "Change Password".

Enter your current password in the previous Password field.

Enter the new password in the "New password" field, then enter it again in the Verify field. If you need to create a secure password, click on the key button next to the "New password" field.

Enter a suggestion to help you remember your password. The suggestion appears if you enter the wrong password three times in succession or if you click on the question mark in the password field of the login window.

Click on "Change Password".

How to connect to a wifi network

You have finally made up your mind! You threw away your old cable-only modem and purchased a new wireless router that will allow you to surf the Internet wirelessly using your laptop, smartphone, video game console and many other devices via the Wi-Fi network .

You did really well, there is no doubt about this. How do you say? You perfectly agree with me, but if you are here now, why can't you understand what needs to be done to connect to a wireless network? Well, but you have absolutely no reason to worry. Again you can count on my help.

I know. For those who are fasting for technology, like you, the use of wireless networks may seem a bit complex, but don't worry because connecting to a wireless network is actually very easy, even for those who do not consider themselves exactly " geniuses ", you have my word. It's all about getting familiar with the router's configuration panel and managing your computer's wireless networks or other devices. It really is a no-brainer!

So give me five minutes of your free time and I will try to explain in a short and, above all, simple way how to connect to a wireless network. I am sure that at the end of this guide you will be more than satisfied and that in case of need you will also be ready to explain to friends, relatives and colleagues in need of help. So, ready? Yes? Great, let's get started right away!

If you want to learn what you need to do to connect to a wireless network, you must first connect your new router to the electrical outlet, to the telephone cable for the Internet connection and to the computer via an Ethernet cable (it only serves for the initial configuration, don't worry!). In addition, if the router in use has a power button, press it so that the device starts working.

Once this is done, if the router has an installation CD, insert it into the computer and follow the instructions on the screen. Otherwise you will have to rely on the old instruction booklet attached to the sales package of the device. In both cases, all you have to do is indicate to the router the type of connection you have and the type of protection you want for your Wi-Fi connection.

To do this, you may need to enter the internal panel of the router by starting the web browser installed on the computer you usually use to surf the net and connecting to the IP address of the modem, typing the latter in the address bar and then clicking the Enter button on the keyboard. Often the modem's IP address is 192.168.1.1 or 192.168.0. In any case, you can find out the IP address of the modem by taking a look at the appropriate label that should be attached to the back of the device or you can try taking a further look at the user manual.

If you are unable to connect to the router's control panel, following the instructions I have just given you, you can easily find out what the right "coordinates" are by following the instructions below.

If you are using a Windows computer you can know the IP address to be able to access the modem control panel by typing cmd in the search field accessible with a click on the Start button on the taskbar or in the appropriate field accessible from the side top right of the Start Screen. Then press Enter to start the program that has been selected automatically. In the window that will open at this point, type the ipconfig command and then press the Enter key on your PC keyboard to get the complete list of addresses related to your connection. The modem's IP address is that series of numbers you see next to the Default gateway item.

If, on the other hand, you are using a Mac, you can find out the IP address through which you can access the modem control panel by clicking on the System Preferences icon (you can find the icon on the Dock, in the Applications folder or you can access it using the Launchpad) and then clicking on Network. In the window that at this point will be shown to you, select the name of the connection in use and click on the Advanced ...

button located at the bottom right. By clicking on the TCP / IP tab you will find the address to which you must connect indicated next to the word Router.

To access the modem control panel, you will also be asked to enter a username and password. Usually the combination to use is admin / admin or admin / password but sometimes you need to use other settings. In this case you can once again take a peek at the modem user manual to find out the correct combination to use.

Proceed now going to configure the password to protect your wireless network in order to prevent unauthorized third parties from happening to the network and exploit the Internet connection without your knowledge. In this regard, I recommend you use a WPA2 / PSK or WPA / AES type key, which is very long and does not make any sense.

Once this step is completed, you must go to the computer to be connected to your new Wi-Fi network and let the computer identify the available connections. Obviously, check that the wireless network indicator is present on the system bar, otherwise it means that you have Wi-Fi disabled on the device in use and therefore you must turn it on by pressing the appropriate button or pushing the appropriate lever.

In the case of Windows PCs, the connection to wireless networks is very simple to implement. All you have to do is click on the network icon in the notification area (next to the clock), select the connection relating to your router and click on the Connect button. Then type the password you previously set for the connection in the Security key field and click OK to establish the connection.

On Mac and more or less the same: you must click on the network icon located in the upper right part of the menu bar, choose one of the available Wi-Fi networks by clicking on it and enter the password to establish the connection.

Even with smartphones and tablets it is possible to connect to a wireless network in an extremely easy way. Both on Android terminals and on iPhone and iPad just go to the Settings menu, press on the Wi-Fi item, select the name of a network and, if necessary, enter the relative password.

Manage Wi-Fi connection on Mac

You can use the Wi-Fi menu on your Mac to view the status of your wireless network connection, switch between networks, or turn Wi-Fi on or off.

Connect to Wi-Fi

You can use the Wi-Fi menu to quickly connect to a nearby wireless network.

Click the Wi-Fi icon or in the menu bar.

If Wi-Fi is turned off, choose "Turn on Wi-Fi".

Select a nearby Wi-Fi network from the list.

If your network isn't listed, make sure it's nearby and others can connect to it. It could also be a "hidden" network. You can connect to a hidden network by choosing "Access another network" and entering the name of the network you are trying to use.
The power of each network in the vicinity is shown next to its name. The greater the number of dark colored signal bars, the greater the power of the network connection.

Please enter your password
For networks with the lock icon next to the name, a password is required. After selecting the network, enter the password when prompted. If you don't know the network password, contact the owner of the Wi-Fi network you are trying to access.

Use a mobile device as a Wi-Fi connection
Depending on the cellular data plan, the iPhone or iPad with Cellular can share its internet connection with the Mac. When the iOS device is configured correctly and is located near the Mac, it is displayed in the Wi-Fi menu as an available connection .

When you select a mobile device as an internet connection, the menu icon changes to indicate that the Mac is currently connected to the device.

Turn Wi-Fi on or off

If you are in an environment where Wi-Fi is not allowed (for example on some airline flights), you can quickly disable Wi-Fi from this menu.

Click on the Wi-Fi icon in the menu bar.

Choose "Turn off Wi-Fi".

When Wi-Fi is turned off, the menu icon changes to an empty indicator. When you can use Wi-Fi again, click the menu icon and choose "Enable Wi-Fi", then connect to the network you want to access if your Mac doesn't connect automatically.

If you don't see the Wi-Fi menu

You can enable and disable the Wi-Fi menu from the Network pane of System Preferences.

From the Apple menu select System Preferences.

Click Network in the System Preferences window.

Select Wi-Fi in the list of available network connections.

Select the "Show Wi-Fi status in the menu bar" option.

Create a network

If you want to create a temporary Wi-Fi connection between your Mac and another device, you can create your network from the Wi-Fi menu.

Click the Wi-Fi menu and choose Create Network. Enter the details of the network, such as a name and a network channel.

When you create a computer-to-computer network, the menu icon changes to show a computer. When finished, click the Wi-Fi menu again and choose Disconnect to close the created network.

Create a folder

You recently bought your first computer and all happy with the thing, you immediately started moving within the operating system to try to clear up your ideas about how it works as much as possible. Good boy! How do you say? You perfectly agree with me but now you would like to know how to create a folder because you are afraid that you could make some mess by yourself? Well, in that case, don't worry ... I can help you.

I know, for you who are at the beginning with the world of information technology, it may seem a little complicated but you have to believe me, creating a folder is an extremely simple operation and reading the indications that I am going to provide you with in the following lines you will immediately make it bill. Regardless of whether you have a computer with the Windows operating system installed or a Mac with OS X, to create a folder it is sufficient to perform a few simple steps. In a few moments you will therefore have generated a "container" to better organize your files and programs.

If you are interested then find out what are the steps that must be taken to create a folder, I suggest that you take a few minutes of free time and focus carefully on reading the indications that I am about to provide you. I am sure that at the end of this guide you will be ready to say that creating a folder was actually a no-brainer.

If you want to find out what operations you need to do in order to create a folder and if you use Windows the first thing you need to do is identify the location on the computer where you want to do this. Depending on what your needs and preferences are, you can in fact create a folder on the desktop or anywhere else on the hard disk. To create a folder on the Windows desktop, simply move to the latter, if instead you want to create a folder elsewhere on the hard disk, press the icon depicting a yellow folder that is attached to the taskbar, then use the labels present on the left sidebar of the displayed window to choose the position in which to act.

Once you have chosen the position in which to create a folder, click with the right mouse button on any empty point, select the New item from the menu that is shown to you and then click on Folder.

After these steps you will see a new folder marked with the default name New folder highlighted in blue. Then type the name you want to assign to the folder with the keyboard and then press the Enter key to apply the changes. When going to rename the folder, keep in mind that the folder names in Windows cannot contain the following special characters:

~
#

%
&
*
{}
\
:
< >
+
|
"

Now that you have finally managed to create a folder on Windows to be able to move text documents, photos, images, music or anything else you want inside you will only have to click with the left mouse button on these elements and, continuing keep the mouse button pressed, drag them to the folder icon that you have just generated.

If instead of moving files within the newly created folder you simply want to copy them, locate the elements on which you intend to act then select them with the mouse by clicking with the left key on the first and then with the left key and the Ctrl key on the others then click right click on any of the files and choose the Copy item from the menu that is shown to you. Now move the mouse over the icon of the newly created folder, right click on it and then select the Paste item from the menu that is shown to you.
Then you can view what you have added inside the folder that you have created by simply double-clicking with the left mouse button on the latter.

Clearly know that despite having taken steps to create a folder on Windows in a specific location, you can always move or copy it where you deem it most appropriate. To move the folder you have just created, click on it with the left mouse button and, keeping it pressed, drag it to the new position. To copy the folder you have just created, click on the latter with the right button of the mousse and choose the Copy item from the menu that is shown to you. Then locate the location where you want to copy the created folder then click anywhere in the new location with the right mouse button and choose the Paste item from the menu that is shown on the screen.

Create a folder on Mac

On the Mac, click the Finder icon in the Dock to open a Finder window, then navigate to the location where you want to create the folder. Alternatively, if you want to create a folder on the desk, click on the desk.

Choose File> New Folder or press Shift-Command-N. If the "New Folder" command is displayed in gray, it means that you cannot create a folder in that location.

Enter a name for the folder, then press Return.

Move items to folders

On the Mac, click the Finder icon in the Dock to open a Finder window.

Do one of the following:

Put an item in the folder: drag it to the folder.
Put multiple items in a folder: select the items, then drag one of the items into the folder. All the selected items move to the folder.
Keep an item in its original position and put a copy in a folder: select the item, hold down the Option key, then drag the item into the folder.
Keep an item in its original position and put an alias for the item in a new folder: hold down the Command and Option keys, then drag the item to the folder to create the alias.
Make a copy of an item in the same folder: select the item, then choose File> duplicate or press Command-D.
Copy files to a different disk: drag the files to the disk.

Move files to a different disk: hold down the Command key, then drag the files to the disk.

Quickly group multiple items into a new folder

You can quickly create a folder of items on your desk or in a Finder window.

On the Mac, select all the items you want to group.

Hold down the Ctrl key while clicking on one of the selected items, then choose "New folder with selection".

Enter a name for the folder, then press Return.

Merge two folders with the same name

If you have two folders with identical names in two different locations, you can merge them into one folder.

On the Mac, hold down the Option key, then drag a folder to the location that contains a folder with the same name. In the dialog that appears, click Merge. The Merge option appears only if one of the folders contains items not present in the other folder. If the folders contain different versions of files with the same name, the only possible options will be Stop or Replace.

Convert pdf files online

Would you like to save a web page in PDF format, so that you can consult it even when you are offline and be able to edit it with notes and annotations? Have you created a series of photos or illustrations that you would like to collect in a single PDF file but don't know how to do it? Don't worry, I'm here today to help you out.

With the guide that you find below, we will discover together how to convert files to PDF for free using the functions included "standard" on your computer as well as excellent applications that allow you to transform Web pages, Office documents, photos and many other types of documents in the format in question. These are zero-cost software, both for Windows and for Mac, capable of doing their job very quickly. Some of them can even be used for commercial purposes!

In the final part of the tutorial we will then take a look at online services thanks to which it is possible to obtain the same results as above without installing programs on the PC. Now, however, let's not lose too much in chatter and let's go straight to the point. So choose the resource that seems most suitable to your needs and start using it following the instructions I am about to give you.

Online services

To conclude in a nice way, as they say, let me tell you about some online services that allow you to convert files to PDF for free. They are multi-platform (they can be used on any operating system and in any browser) and protect user privacy by deleting all the files that are uploaded to their servers within hours of uploading.

CloudConvert

Another great web tool you can use to convert your files to PDF for free is CloudConvert. It is a "universal" online converter that does not appear to be focused on PDFs such as SmallPDF, but also allows to transform a very wide range of files in this format. It has an upload limit of 100 MB which can be raised to 1 GB if you create a free account on the site.

To use it, connected to its home page https://cloudconvert.com/anything-to-pdf and drag the documents to convert to PDF in the browser window.

If, on the other hand, you want to select the files to be manually edited, click on the Select Files button. If then the files you want to transform into PDF are on the network, press the adjacent arrow and select, from the menu you see appear, the option to upload them via URL or via one of the supported cloud storage services.

Then click on the Start conversion button. Then wait for the documents to be processed and download their version in PDF format by pressing the Download button that appears next to their names. If you want to download all the converted files at the same time, press the create archive button at the bottom and select the compressed archive format you want to obtain as the last file from the menu that opens.

I also point out that if you want, you can merge two or more files into a single PDF document. Just select the PDF item from the combine all into one drop-down menu located at the bottom right instead of clicking on the Start conversion button.

Virtual PDF printer

If you want to convert a Web page, a Word document or any other type of printable file to PDF, rely on a virtual printer. Virtual printers are software that, as deduced from the name itself, once installed, are viewed by the system as if they were real printers.

This allows them to be used in all applications that support the sending of print commands to printers: work suites, web browsers, email clients, graphics software and so on. The newer versions of Windows and Mac already include them, but if you want you can download others for free from the Internet. Read on if you want to know more.

Windows

If you use Windows 10, you can convert any type of printable document to a PDF using the virtual printer included by default in the operating system. All you have to do is display the content you want to convert to PDF on the screen (e.g. a web page, a photo or a document), find the command to print from the File menu and select Microsoft Print to PDF from the list of printers available.

If you are using a older version of Windows, however, you can rely on virtual printers produced by third parties. Among the best in the free sector, I would like to point out doPDF which can be used at no cost even for commercial purposes.

To download doPDF to your computer, connected to the official website of the software and click on the Download now button! twice in a row.

When the download is complete, open the dopdf – full.exe file you just got on your PC, deselect the Install add-in for Microsoft Office option from the window that opens (it is a function that allows you to add a quick link to DoPDF in Office, there is no need), remove (if you want) also check the box for sending anonymous statistics which is at the bottom right and complete the setup by clicking first on Install now and then on Yes, on OK and Close.

When installation is complete, open the document you want to transform into PDF, click the Print ... command from the File menu and select doPDF from the list of available printers.

Then click on the Print button and select the quality of the document to be obtained from the window that opens (Best quality for maximum quality, Medium for intermediate quality and Smallest file for minimum quality). To finish, click on the Browse button, choose the folder in which to save the PDF and press the OK button to start creating the document.

Mac

All newer versions of macOS also include a virtual PDF printer. This means that if you use a Mac you can convert your files to PDF for free starting from any printable document without having to download additional applications from the Internet.
All you have to do is open the Web page, the document or the photo you want to transform into PDF, select the Print ... command from the File menu and select the Save as PDF item from the drop-down menu located at the bottom left. Then choose the folder in which to export the document, click on the Save button and you're done.

Applications to convert images to PDF

Would you like to group a series of JPG, PNG or TIFF images into a single PDF file but you don't know how to do it? Don't worry, now I'm going to point out a couple of applications for Windows and Mac that should be right for you. You find them shown below.

PDFill FREE PDF Tools (Windows)

If you are using a PC with Windows installed (any version), the suggestion I feel I can give you is to turn to PDFill FREE PDF Tools. It is a suite of tools for editing and converting PDF documents that can be used for free for both personal and commercial purposes.

To download it to your PC, connected to its official website and click first on the Download link located on the left, then on the Download now button under the word GET FREE Basic Version on the page that opens and on the additional Download Now button.

Once the download is complete, open the PDFill_FREE_PDF_Tools_Editor_Basic.exe file on your PC and just click on the Yes button and then on Next. Then put the check mark next to the item I accept the terms in the License Agreement and complete the setup by clicking in sequence on the Next buttons three consecutive times, on Install and on Finish.

If during the installation process you are asked to install GhostScript and the .Net Framework, accept. These are two free software without which it would not be possible to use many of the functions included in PDFill FREE PDF Tools (they are not promotional content, quiet).
Now you can take action! Once the setup is complete, start PDFill FREE PDF Tools by double clicking on the relative icon that has been added to the desktop and, after viewing the

program window, start the tool to convert images to PDF by clicking on the Convert images to PDF button.

Then drag the images to be included in the PDF into the window that opens or click on the Add an Image button at the top and select them "manually". If you then want to add an entire folder of images, press the Add all Images under a Folder button and select it from there.
Now put the selected images in the order you prefer using the Move Up (move up) and Move Down (move down) buttons that are on the right and finally click on the Save as ... button, so as to save the final PDF in a folder of your choice.

If you have special needs, before proceeding with the conversion you can also intervene on the settings relating to the final file using the specific options and menus that you find in the lower part of the window. For example, you can define the layout, orientation etc.

Preview (Mac)

If you use a Mac, you can instead transform your images into PDF using Preview, the application for viewing photos and PDF included by default in macOS. All you have to do is open the first image you want to include in your document and call the left sidebar with thumbnails from the View menu located at the top.
Then you have to drag all the images to be inserted into the PDF in the bar that appeared laterally, you have to arrange them in the order you prefer (using the mouse) and you have to "print" them in PDF as we have seen previously. So, you have to select the Print ... command from the File menu and then you have to select the Save as PDF item from the drop-down menu located at the bottom left.

Create and manage an account

Windows 8.1

Create a Microsoft account

Swipe in from the right edge of the screen and tap Settings, then tap Change PC settings. If you use the mouse, place the pointer in the lower right corner of the screen, move it up, click Settings and then click Change PC settings.

Tap or click Accounts and then Other Accounts.

Tap or click Add an account.

Enter your account info to allow this person to log into Windows. You can do it in four ways:

If the person you want to add already has a Microsoft account, enter it.
If the person to be added does not have a Microsoft account, you can use their email address to create one. Enter the email address this person uses most often.
If the person you want to add doesn't have an email address, tap or click Sign up to get a new email address. Free.
If the person to add is a child, tap or click Add a child account.

Follow the instructions to complete the account setup.

Create a local account

Swipe in from the right edge of the screen and tap Settings, then tap Change PC settings.

If you use the mouse, position the pointer in the lower right corner of the screen, move it up, click Settings and then click Change PC settings.

Tap or click Accounts and then Other Accounts.

Tap or click Add an account and then Sign in without a Microsoft account (not recommended).

Tap or click Local account.

Please enter a username for the new account.

If you want this person to log in with a password, enter the password and confirm it, add a password hint and then tap or click Next.

If your PC is part of a domain, your domain's security settings may allow you to skip this step and simply tap or click Next if you prefer.

Tap or click Finish.

Windows 7

My computer is included in a domain

Open Microsoft Management Console by clicking the Start button, typing mmc in the search box, and then pressing ENTER. If you are asked to specify an administrator password or a confirmation, type the password or enter the confirmation.

In the left pane of Microsoft Management Console, click Local Users and Groups.

If you don't see Local Users and Groups, the snap-in may not have been added to the Microsoft Management Console. Do the following to install it:

In the Microsoft Management Console, choose Add / Remove Snap-in from the File menu.

Click Local Users and Groups and then click Add.

Click Local Computer, click Finish, and then click OK.

Click on the Users folder.

Click Action and then New User.

Type the appropriate information in the dialog and then click Create.

When you're done creating user accounts, click Close.

My computer is included in a workgroup

To open User Accounts, click the Start button, click Control Panel, then User Accounts and Family Safety, and then click User Accounts.

Click Manage another account. If you are asked to specify an administrator password or a confirmation, type the password or enter the confirmation.

Click Create a new account.

Type the name you want to assign to the user account, click an account type and then click Create account.

Create accounts on MAC

Add a user

On the Mac, choose Apple menu> System Preferences, then click Users and Groups.
Click the Padlock icon to open it.

Enter an administrator name and password.

Click the Add + button below the list of users.

Click the New Account pop-up menu, then choose a user type.

Administrator: an administrator can add and manage other users, install apps and change settings. The new user you create the first time you set up Mac is an administrator. Mac can have multiple administrators. You can create new ones or convert standard users to administrators. Do not set up automatic login for an administrator. Otherwise someone could restart Mac and log in with administrator privileges. To protect Mac, don't reveal the administrator name and password to anyone.

Standard: Standard users are configured by an administrator. Standard users can install apps and change their settings, but cannot add other users or change their settings.

Sharing only: Share-only users can access shared files remotely, but cannot log in or change computer settings. To allow the user to access your shared files or the screen, you may need to change the settings in the "File Sharing", "Screen Sharing" or "Remote Management" pane of the Sharing preferences. V

For more information on the options available for each type of user, click the Help button in the lower left corner of the dialog.

Enter a full name for the new user. An account name is automatically generated. To use a different account name, enter it now: you cannot change it later.

Enter a password for the user, then enter it again for verification. Enter a suggestion to help the user remember their password.

Click "Create user".

Depending on the type of user you create, you can also do one of the following:

For an administrator, select "User can administer this computer".
Use Sharing preferences to specify whether the user can share your files and your screen.

If the Mac has Touch ID, a new user can add a fingerprint after logging in to the Mac. The user can then use Touch ID to unlock the Mac and password protected items and to purchase items on iTunes Store, App Store and Apple Books using your Apple ID.

Convert a standard user into an administrator

On the Mac, choose Apple menu> System Preferences, then click Users and Groups.
Click the Padlock icon to open it.

Enter an administrator name and password.

Select a standard or managed user from the list of users, then select "User can administer this computer".

How to create a Word document

Every time you write a document in Word, do you waste a lot of time to set the sheet as you like, with your favorite writing font, certain margins and certain spaces for the lines? Evidently you have never heard of Word templates.

Word templates can be used to create documents with a different style from the default of the program without having to waste time setting the worksheet, characters and spaces differently each time. Discover with me how to make a model with Word and you will save a lot of precious time.

For the tutorial I will use the version of Word included in Office 2019. Having said that, the indications in the article should be valid for all the most recent versions of Word, from 2007 onwards, both for Windows and for macOS. In addition, I will also mention the possibility of using templates in Word Online (the Web based version of the famous Microsoft software) and in Word apps for smartphones and tablets. Happy reading and good work!
If you want to learn how to make a model with Word on your PC, the first step you need to take is to start the program through its link in the Windows Start menu or in the macOS Launchpad and start editing the worksheet by setting the features that you prefer.

Then click with the right mouse button anywhere on the sheet and select the Font item from the menu that appears to select the writing font to be used by default instead of the standard one in Word. You can choose the font, its size and apply effects such as strikethrough, all uppercase etc. (although I don't think you want to make documents with all text struck through or formatted in another particular way by default). In addition, by clicking on the Text Effects button (available only on Windows), you can set a fill or add an outline to the typed text.

By moving to the Advanced tab, then, you can set parameters such as character spacing. Once you have made all the changes you want, to save them, click on the OK button.
Now you have to customize all the other parameters of the worksheet. Then, make a new right click anywhere in the document and select the Paragraph item from the menu that appears.

In the window that opens, use the Alignment menu to set the type of default alignment to be given to the text, the fields located under the Indents heading to set the indents to the left and right of the text, the fields located under the Spacing entry to set the spacing before and after text, the Leading drop-down menu to adjust the size of the leading and so on.

Then move to the Text Distribution tab and use the boxes in the latter to adjust the various pagination settings and choose whether to omit the line numbers and disable the hyphenation
In addition, I point out that by clicking on the Tabs button located at the bottom, you can adjust the tabs of the document. When you have adjusted all your preferences, click on the OK button to save them.

Another thing you can do is change the margins of the sheet using the ruler tool, which can be easily enabled by going to the Word View tab, clicking on the Show button and checking the Ruler option. If you deem it appropriate, you can also create letterhead by inserting a logo and / or background in your document.
When you're done adjusting all the parameters of your worksheet, you're ready to turn the newly created document into a template. If you use Windows, then click on the File button located at the top left, select the Save As item from the menu that appears and then choose the Browse option that appears on the screen.

In the window that opens later, select Word Template or Word 97-2003 Template (if you want to create a model perfectly compatible even with versions of Office prior to 2007) from the Save As drop-down menu: in this way, you will be automatically redirected in the path where the customized Word templates are saved (Documents> Custom Office Templates) and save your template by typing the name you want to give in the File name field and clicking on the Save button.

Mac

To save your custom Word template, go to the File menu (top left) and select the Save as template item from the latter. In the window that opens, select the Microsoft Word Model option or the Microsoft Word 97 - 2004 Model option (if you want to make the model usable in older versions of the program), make sure that the Located in drop-down menu is selected the Word templates folder (Users / your name / Library / Group Containers / UBF8T346G9.Office / User Content.localized / Templates.localized), type the name you want to assign to the file in the appropriate text field and click on the Save button to complete the operation.

From this moment on, you can recall your customized template in Word at any time by opening the program, going to the menu File> New (or File> New from model, if you use a Mac), selecting the Personal tab and clicking on the file preview. Comfortable, right?

Note: as you have surely noticed, the Word Character and Paragraph menus also have a button called Set as default (bottom center) which, if clicked, allows you to use the current settings as Word default settings without having to create a new template . It's up to you to choose the road you find most comfortable. I, however, advise you to leave the default settings of Word as they are and to act on a custom model created by you, to be recalled if necessary (as I have explained to you before).

How to manage email with Gmail

(I list this provider because I believe it is worthy of being presented as the best (in my opinion) in terms of safety, speed and user friendly).

Gmail is the email service offered and managed by Google. It is compatible with most browsers and email clients for PCs, smartphones and tablets. In addition, in the mobile field, it is available through special apps for Android and iOS.
It has a large number of features aimed at optimal management of e-mail: extremely advanced spam filters, automatic detection and blocking of harmful / harmful emails, the possibility of setting custom filters and blocks, integration with third-party add-ons and much more. even more.

Having a Gmail account doesn't just mean having a functional email box. In fact, the same profile can be used to access the entire range of services offered by Google: Google Drive and Google Docs, Google Photos, YouTube, Maps, Play Store, Play Music, Play Film etc. etc.

In its free version, Gmail offers 15 GB of shared space between the various services, which can be easily increased by purchasing additional packages. There is also a professional version of Gmail, included in the G-Suite package, specifically designed for companies, and which has, among the additional features, collaborative tools and greater availability of storage space. In other words, Gmail is not just an email account, but a real access key to the entire range of services provided by "big G"!

In the subsequent bars of this guide, however, I will focus my attention exclusively on the functioning of Gmail's email on the various platforms with which it is compatible: Android, iOS (therefore iPhone) and PC (Web and client).
If you do not yet have a free account on Gmail, you can create it in an extremely simple way, through the platform that you consider most appropriate (smartphone, tablet, PC and so on).

If you intend to use Gmail via your computer, know that you can follow at least two different paths: use the Webmail made available by Google, accessible through any browser, or configure e-mail in a special program, such as Windows 10 or Apple Mail MacOS mail.

To access Google's e-mail via browser, do the following: first, connect to this web page https://mail.google.com/mail/u/0/ your e-mail address in the appropriate field, press the Enter key on the keyboard, then enter the access password in the next field and you're done.

If everything went the right way, after a few moments you should have access to your mailbox. As you have certainly noticed, the Gmail web interface is extremely intuitive: through the left navigation bar, you can access the various folders of the mailbox (e.g. incoming mail, important messages, sent mail, the spam, trash, outgoing mail etc. etc.).

The content of the inbox folder is shown in the center of the screen which, as you can see, is divided into different tabs, which contain the various categories of messages (which Google is able to recognize thanks to artificial intelligence). If you do not like this behavior and would like all messages to be displayed in the Inbox without any division, you can deactivate the tab division in the following way: click on the □ button located at the top right, select the Configure mailbox item from the menu shown on the screen and remove the check mark from all the available boxes, except for the Main tab. To conclude and save the changes, click on the Save button.

Always through the same menu, you can adjust the display format of the e-mail, its settings and add new graphic themes. If you wish, you can also expand Gmail Web with a series of add-ons, useful for integrating Google's email with other services: to use it, click on the Install add-ons item in the aforementioned menu (or on the (+) button in the right bar of the Gmail interface), locate the component of your interest and, after clicking on its preview, press the Install button to add it.

The operation of Gmail Web is extremely simple: you can compose a new message by clicking on the (+) Write button located in the upper left corner of the screen, reply to a message already present by pressing the Reply button located at the bottom of the itself and access the operations that can be performed on messages (deleting, archiving, transferring from one folder to another and much more) using either a practical menu, accessible by right-clicking on the preview of the message of your interest, or by using the buttons in the window of Gmail, displayed at the top of already opened messages.

Furthermore, through the search bar located at the top of the page, you can quickly search for emails based on sender, recipient, subject, size and many other parameters.

Conclusion

Well, so here we are, it seems that we have ended our "journey" together.
I sincerely hope that this mini guide can help you in your daily routine whether it's for work or hobby.

Maybe now, the things that previously seemed completely "alien" will sound a little more familiar to you.
I really hope that this book will solve the problems of as many people as possible, and that in turn they will be able to transmit what they have learned between these pages to friends and other people.

A greetings,
Alessandro Lazzara.